j394.2 Baldwin, Margaret
BA
Thanksgiving

| DATE | | |
|------|------|------|
| NOV. 23 1983 NOV 1 3 '95 | | |
| DEC 0 1 1984 NOV 29 '95 | | |
| DEC. 0 2 1985 DEC 23 '00 | | |
| | NO 24 '00 | |
| DE 6 '85 | DE 04 '06 | |
| DE 1 0 '86 NO 2 7 '09 | | |
| NO 7 '87 | | |
| NO 23 '87 | | |
| NO 14 '91 | | |
| DEC 8 '93 | | |
| NOV 30 '90 | | |

© THE BAKER & TAYLOR CO.

# THANKSGIVING

# MARGARET BALDWIN

# THANKSGIVING

**FRANKLIN WATTS**
*New York / London / Toronto / Sydney / 1983*
**A FIRST BOOK**

Illustrations by Anne Canevari Green

Photographs courtesy of:
Religious News Service: pp. 4, 16, 20, 38;
Library of Congress: p. 13;
New York Public Library Picture Collection:
pp. 23, 24, 27, 30, 35;
Macy's: p. 47

Library of Congress Cataloging in Publication Data

Baldwin, Margaret, 1948-
Thanksgiving.

(A First book)
Includes index.
Summary: Describes the Pilgrims' arrival and
early life, the "first Thanksgiving," and the
development of that harvest festival into the
holiday it is today. Includes recipes and games.
1. Thanksgiving Day—Juvenile literature.
[1. Thanksgiving Day]
I. Green, Anne Canevari, ill.   II. Title.
GT4975.B34 1983        394.2'683        82-16005
ISBN 0-531-04532-3

# CONTENTS

*Dedicated to the memory of my great-aunt,*
*Mary Reeves, who made my Thanksgivings*
*some of the best times of my childhood,*
*times I shall remember always.*

# 1

# THANKSGIVING

When you sit down to Thanksgiving dinner with your family and friends, you are practicing one of the oldest customs of the human race. The Thanksgiving we celebrate today is, in many ways, a harvest festival. We give thanks for the food we have to eat and for our families. If there are friends or family members who can't be with us, we think about them and hope they are having a happy Thanksgiving, too. In many ways our Thanksgiving celebration is similar to festivals of early times.

The ancient Greeks celebrated thanksgiving festivals throughout the year to give thanks for many different things. The Greeks believed in gods and goddesses who were very much like human beings. These gods and goddesses had human feelings. The Greeks thought their gods could be bad-tempered and angry, happy and playful, and sad and sulky, just as humans could be. They believed the gods ruled the lives of men and women. If someone pleased the gods and goddesses, they would give him or her a happy, healthy life. But if someone didn't please the gods, the Greeks believed their gods would be angry and punish them. Therefore, it was a good idea to keep the gods pleased. Thus, the ancient Greeks said "thank you" to their gods and goddesses for every good event of their lives. A general who won a war held a thanksgiving festival with his soldiers. A person traveling from one city to another gave the gods a "thank-you offering" if he or she had a safe journey.

The ancient Greeks also celebrated a festival at harvest time, as did men and women all over the world. They worked hard all spring and summer raising crops so that they would have food to eat and to sell to their neighbors. The money they earned bought more food, clothing, and shelter for their families.

Crops need sunshine and rain to grow, and the Greeks believed their gods and goddesses made the sun shine and rain fall. If the gods were angry, it might not rain at all, and the crops would dry up and die. The gods might also cause it to rain too much, and there would be flooding. But if the gods and goddesses were happy, it would be a beautiful summer. The crops would grow, and everyone could face the harsh winter with enough food. Every year, after a good harvest, the Greeks held a harvest festival. This festival was to thank the gods and goddesses for the food and all the blessings the gods had given during the year. It was so important, armies at war would stop fighting to share in the celebration.

The ancient Greeks were not the only people who held thanksgiving celebrations. The Bible has many stories about how the Hebrews offered thanks to God. They celebrated the Feast of the Tabernacles in October to mark the end of the farming season, when everything the people had grown or raised was gathered in. The celebration lasted seven days and was a time of feasting and merriment. People camped out under booths made of branches, in memory of the shelters they had used during their wandering through the desert. These booths were called *tabernacles*.

In the following passage, Moses, their leader, tells the Hebrews how to celebrate the Feast of the Tabernacles. As you can see, it is very much like our Thanksgiving:

"Thou shalt keep the Feast of the Tabernacles seven days, after that thou hast gathered in from thy threshing floor and from thy wine press; and thou shalt rejoice in thy feast, thou, and thy son and thy daughter, and thy manservant and thy maidservant, and the Levite and the stranger, and the fatherless, and the widow that are within thy gates. Seven days shalt thou keep a feast unto the Lord thy God . . . " (Deuteronomy 16: 13, 14, 15).

During the Middle Ages, England and Europe kept the tradition of the harvest festival celebration. The festival in England was known as "Harvest Home," and it began when the last load of grain was carted into the barn. Everyone in the village went to the fields and decorated the last load with ribbons and flowers. As the horses or oxen dragged the wagon to the barn, the people danced around it, singing songs of thanks. After the final load was stored away, there were parties with feasting and merriment. These were the last parties before the cold, cruel days of winter.

As you can see, men and women have celebrated the harvest festival for many, many years. We still celebrate it today. But Thanksgiving has an extra-special meaning for Americans. It is a time to give thanks for *freedom* as well as for the blessings of nature. For our Thanksgiving commemorates a small group of men, women, and children who left their homes in England long ago and traveled across the Atlantic Ocean to a new land.

They went in search of freedom. They faced many dangers, and many of them died. It is the memory of this small group—the Pilgrims—that makes our Thanksgiving different from the thanksgiving celebrations of other cultures.

Who were the Pilgrims? Why did they make the long and difficult journey to America?

*Two youngsters dressed in Pilgrims' clothes leave church. Our country's founders came to the New World in search of religious freedom.*

# 2

# SEARCHING
# FOR
# FREEDOM

Religious freedom—what does that mean to you?

In America, people can attend the church or temple they want to attend. No one—including the government—has the right to tell us how to worship. What a shock it would be if our minister or rabbi was arrested and taken to prison! What if your parents or someone you know were fired from their jobs because they belong to a certain religious faith? This is what happened to those people we now call the Pilgrims. They lived in England during the 1600s and were known as the *Separatists*, because they had "separated" from the Church of England.

At that time the Church of England ruled all aspects of a citizen's life and worked closely with the government. Bishops and other top church officials were powerful political figures. The king or queen was the ruler of the church as well as ruler of the country.

Church ceremonies were filled with the music of organ and choirs, the priests wore beautiful, expensive robes, and the churches were decorated with ornaments of gold and stained glass. In big cities, the churches were often soaring cathedrals.

Some people felt that these churches had wealth and power, but that they had forgotten about God. They felt that religion had become nothing more than a sweetly singing choir or a huge new pipe organ or beautiful stained-glass windows. The needs of the poor, sick, and helpless had been forgotten.

Religious holidays, such as Christmas, seemed to be occasions for drunken parties, dancing, and greedy feasting instead of the celebration of the birth of Christ. This was true not only in England, but in Europe as well.

A few people came forward and said this was not the way God wanted people to worship Him. They separated, or broke away from, the organized churches of the day and formed their own churches. They became known as Separatists. Their religious customs were very different from those of the churches they were protesting. Their houses of worship were made of plain material without decoration. There was no organ music (which they called the Devil's bagpipes!). Some congregations stood for prayers, instead of kneeling. Prayers often lasted several hours.

Religious holidays were times for prayer and solemn thought, not laughing, parties, and games. They were times for *fasting*, which meant the people ate no food and drank only water for at least a day. The Separatists wore plain clothing, lived simply, and worked hard. They were devoted to helping the poor.

Remember that the Church of England was closely tied to the government. To be against the Church of England was also seen as being opposed to the king. Thus, the Separatists came to be looked upon as traitors—when in reality they simply wanted to practice their own religious beliefs. They were fired from government jobs, spied upon, and sometimes even arrested and thrown into prison. They believed in turning the other cheek instead of fighting back, however, and so they decided to move to another country. They chose Holland where there was freedom of thought and expression.

The Separatists saw their move to Holland as a *pilgrimage*. A pilgrimage is a journey for religious reasons. If you travel to Bethlehem, for example, to visit Christ's birthplace, you are making a pilgrimage to Bethlehem. The Separatists were traveling to Holland to worship the way they believed God wanted them to worship. They came to be known as *Pilgrims* because they considered their journey to be a religious pilgrimage.

The move was not easy. The Pilgrims had to leave their families, friends, homes, and jobs. They were going to a land where the language was different. What was worse, they had to sneak out of England.

The first time the Pilgrims tried to escape, the ship's captain informed the authorities. The Pilgrims were arrested and searched. Several of the men spent months in prison before they were released and told not to try to leave again. The next spring, in 1608, the Pilgrims tried once again to escape from England. The men got safely aboard ship when suddenly a troop of armed soldiers galloped out of the woods and arrested the women and children remaining on shore.

At the sight of the soldiers, the ship's captain, fearing arrest, took up the anchor and the ship sailed off. The Pilgrim men begged with tears in their eyes to be taken back to their families, left in the hands of the soldiers. The Dutch captain refused and sailed to Holland. The British government, left with starving women and children on their hands, decided to send them off to join their husbands and fathers in Amsterdam, Holland, where they found another group of Separatists already living. Unfortunately, the two groups could not get along. Therefore, the Pilgrim leaders, John Robinson and William Brewster, decided to move the group to Leyden, Holland.

The Pilgrims lived in Holland for twelve years. Life was not easy, even though the Dutch never interfered in their religious practices. Work was hard with little pay. People began falling sick, especially the children. And the Pilgrims were still English at heart, despite their dispute over religious beliefs. They saw with dismay that their children were growing up Dutch—speaking a strange language and learning Dutch customs. Some of the older children were even breaking away from their parents' beliefs. The city of Leyden was full of temptations—parties and merrymaking. Further, the Dutch regarded Sunday, or the Sabbath, as a holiday. The Pilgrims, on the other hand, stayed in church for hours, praying devoutly. The children were expected to be very quiet and well-behaved. After church, the Pilgrims spent the day praying and fasting at home. The Pilgrim children wanted to do what their Dutch friends were doing. The Pilgrims saw that unless they left Holland, their children might lose their religion and their English background. But the Pilgrims could not return to England. Where could they go?

At that time, there were reports of a new land across the Atlantic Ocean—America. Explorers and adventurers had been to the American continent and were returning with strange and wonderful tales. There were miraculous plants: corn, which could produce a crop three times a year and could be used to make everything from puddings to bread; and tobacco, which was regarded then as a kind of wonder drug. The Indians who lived in America were reported to be friendly, and it was even said that they worshiped the white people. There were mountains of gold, rivers of silver, and "fountains of youth." Fish were abundant, and fur-bearing animals filled the wilderness. It seemed an ideal location.

The Pilgrims decided to sail to the New World. But they knew their journey would not be easy. They needed a ship to take them across the vast ocean. They needed money for supplies. They needed food and clothes for the long voyage. Who would supply the money? The Pilgrims barely had enough to live on. None of them could afford the enormous expense of making such a long journey. They decided to look for *sponsors*—people to loan them the money they needed to make the trip to America. The Pilgrims planned to pay the sponsors back with the money they hoped to earn in America through fishing and fur-trapping. Several Pilgrims returned to England to find sponsors and make arrangements for the trip.

# 3

# PACKING

The Pilgrims found sponsors who drew up a *charter*. A charter is an agreement between two parties, in this case the Pilgrims and a group known as the Merchant Adventurers. The two parties agreed that the Adventurers would provide the money for the trip and the Pilgrims would provide the people. It was a standard charter of the time, giving the Pilgrims 80,000 acres (32,400 hectares) of land with fishing rights and permission to trade with the Indians. The colonies would be self-governing, and they even promised to respect the bishops of the Church of England (although they carefully left out the word "obey"). The Pilgrims agreed to send back fish and furs and anything else the Adventurers could sell. They received the king's (James I) permission to leave England. All seemed ready.

But there were delays. The sponsors began to argue. The Pilgrims became mistrustful of the men that were representing them in England. Finally, a copy of the charter was sent to Leyden. Then a difficult decision had to be made: who should go and who had to stay behind? Far more wanted to go than could fit into two ships. Those who could be ready soonest would be allowed to go.

Two ships were to make the voyage—the *Speedwell* and a larger ship, the *Mayflower*. On Saturday, July 22, 1620, the sixty-six men, women, and children who were chosen to go to the New World left in the ship, *Speedwell*. They were to meet the *Mayflower* in England. Most of those who parted in Leyden that day believed they would never see each other again. One of the ministers who was staying behind knelt. Those aboard ship and those left on land knelt with him. He called for heaven's blessing and God's protection for those sailing. Tears ran down his cheeks, and soon all the Pilgrims were weeping. Even the curious Dutch bystanders began to cry, they were so touched by the farewell. The tide was favorable, and the wind was fair. The ship raised anchor and sailed away. Within four days, the *Speedwell* reached England and was joined by the *Mayflower*.

What would you take with you if you were going off to a new land? Look around you. Think of everything that is essential to your survival. You couldn't just run to the store for a bottle of milk. You might be in the New World long months before another ship arrived from home. Your ship is small. You don't have much room to pack things. What you would decide to take and what the Pilgrims took are probably very similar.

Clothes, of course, were very important. The Pilgrims needed clothes for a cold climate. They took dresses, shirts, trousers, hats, stockings, and underwear. Coats and cloaks were packed. One man, William Mullins, took 126 pairs of shoes and 13 pairs of boots!

The Pilgrims knew that there was plenty of wood for building shelter in the New World, so they took tools. They intended to build nineteen cottages as a start. They also took chairs, tables, beds, cradles, and cupboards. Chests, spinning wheels, looms, rugs, and mattresses were also stowed in the

*The Pilgrims left Leyden on July 22, 1620.*

ship's hold. Cooking utensils were important. They took pots, pans, and skillets, knives and spoons (forks hadn't come into use yet), and pewter plates and mugs. They took hourglasses and sundials. They took candlesticks, buckets, and pails.

The Pilgrims also took guns and other weapons with them to the New World. They knew they would need the muskets and fowling pieces (guns for shooting birds) for hunting food. They also packed gunpowder and shot. For defense of the colony the Pilgrims brought armor, helmets, and several small cannons. But they hoped to make friends with the Indians, instead of fighting with them, so they took along stores of trading goods—bracelets, beads, rings, knives, and red and blue cloth.

Some of their most precious possessions were books. After all, you could make a new table or chair, or grow food—but where could you get books? The Pilgrims took their Bibles, of course, and Psalmbooks. There were *hornbooks* and Bible stories for the children. A hornbook was made of a sheet of paper on which was written the alphabet or numbers. The paper was mounted on a small board covered with a piece of clear horn from the antlers of a deer. The horn protected the paper from damage. The Pilgrims also took calendars and almanacs. Dr. Samuel Fuller took medical books, and Captain Miles Standish brought along *Caesar's Commentaries* and a history of the world.

How could you travel anywhere and leave your dog behind? You couldn't—and the Pilgrims couldn't leave their pets behind either. Several dogs, cats, and even caged birds made the voyage. Of all the animals, the cats enjoyed the trip the most. Storing food for long periods of time in a ship makes it an ideal place for mice and rats to live. Almost all English ships carried an official ship's cat to reduce the rodent population. Thus the *Mayflower's* cats were useful and able to feed themselves as well.

Food was a problem because there were no refrigerators. How could food be kept from spoiling? The Pilgrims took smoked meat—beef, pork, and herring—which keeps for a long time without spoiling. Eggs were hardboiled and then pickled. There was also lemon juice. Sailors didn't know what vitamin C was, but they knew that lemons somehow prevented the dreaded disease scurvy. There were casks of flour, oatmeal, and butter. Spices were very important because none of these would be found in the New World: cinnamon, nutmeg, pepper, and salt. Live animals were taken aboard—pigs, goats, chickens, sheep, and rabbits. Some of these were killed and eaten on board ship. Others were used to start herds in the New World.

The Pilgrims knew they would have to face many problems on the ocean voyage itself. But there would be additional problems and other dangers to face once they reached the New World. The Pilgrims discovered, before they left, that all the wonderful stories they had heard about America were greatly exaggerated. They heard tales of terrifying animals that lurked in the woods. Some said the Indians were cannibals. It was reported that there were terrible storms and the winters were harsh. It was said that disease had spread across the ocean. Medical knowledge was crude, and in the New World there would be no hospitals. There might not be any drinkable water. (The Pilgrims carried stores of beer, brandy, and wine in case there wasn't.) What food they took might have to last for months after they landed.

The Pilgrims knew all the dangers they faced—real or imaginary—but they were determined to sail anyway. Freedom was more important to them than life itself.

*The* Mayflower

# 4

# CASTING FATE
# TO THE WIND

The Pilgrims trusted that their ship's crew would get them to their destination, which was Virginia. But navigation was crude in those days. The ship's pilot steered by stars, compass, and a few other instruments. There were no accurate charts for the route across the Atlantic. The pilot knew only that America lay to the west and that he had to cross a vast, storm-tossed ocean to get there. He had a vague idea of what the land looked like and some idea of how long the voyage would take—but that was all. The Pilgrims truly cast their fate to the wind—for a ship could be blown off course in a storm or becalmed for days while precious supplies were used up.

The two ships started out in August 1620, after many delays. It soon became apparent that the *Speedwell* would never last the whole trip. The ship leaked badly. After putting in at Plymouth, England, for repairs, the Pilgrims decided that only the smaller *Mayflower* would make the voyage. Several people chose to stay in England because the journey from Holland had been very difficult.

The Pilgrims were faced with a new problem. Summer was gone, and the treacherous fall storms in the Atlantic were beginning. The crossing would have been bad enough in the summer. Several people urged the Pilgrims to abandon their attempt to reach the New World, at least until the following spring. But by then the stores would be used up and there would be no money to buy more. The Pilgrims decided to take the risk and sail. On September 6, 1620, the tiny ship with its cargo of 102 men, women, and children, plus dogs, cats, birds, and other livestock set sail.

Food was rationed. Each person was allowed only so much a day. Water was also strictly rationed, for people can live without food for a long time but only for a few days without water. Cooking had to be done in "fireboxes" below deck where the Pilgrims lived. A "firebox" was an iron tray filled with sand on which a fire could be built. In the wooden ships, fire was very dangerous. Food was cooked under careful supervision for small groups of people at a time.

There were other problems with the food. Have you ever had to throw out flour because it had bugs in it? These are called weevils. These bugs, which are a type of beetle, get into flour or meal after a short period of time. If you are at sea, you cannot just throw out the flour. The weevils get into bread and biscuits, too. But the people had to eat them. The sailors were used to the weevils. They took their biscuits and rapped them on the table until the little bugs ran out! Then they would eat the biscuits. But this must have been difficult for the Pilgrims to swallow.

Sanitation was a problem. There were no toilets (or "heads" as they are now called aboard ship). Wastes were washed down into the bottom of the ship. The smell was terrible below deck, where the Pilgrims lived in cramped conditions. Many people were seasick, and that added to the stench. And wherever there is filth, there is the danger of disease.

What was it like on that small ship?

To find out, go into your bedroom. Take a tape measure and measure 5 feet (1.5 m) up from the floor. That was where the overhead (the ceiling below deck) was located. Anyone over 5 feet (1.5 m) tall had to hunch over. (Remember, however, that people were smaller on the average than we are today.) Do you have a standard-size, single bed? If so, sit down on it. Now you have some idea of how much room each grown person had on the *Mayflower*. Every adult was allotted about the same amount of space as your bed occupies. In the small space your bed takes up, with the overhead only a few feet above, they had to cook all their meals, take care of the children, store their possessions, and spend most of their time. Sit on your bed for an hour and imagine being trapped there, below deck, smelling terrible odors for nine and a half weeks. That is how long it took the *Mayflower* to cross the Atlantic.

Imagine, too, that every few minutes someone heaves a bucket of icy cold water over you, and that the ship is pitching and rolling so badly you have to be lashed to your bed to keep from falling out. The *Mayflower* ran into storms in the Atlantic. Great waves of chilled water splashed over the deck, soaking everyone and everything on board. Clothes were never dry and the chill ate into people's bones. It was impossible to rest. The noise was earsplitting. The tiny ship rattled and creaked, and the flapping sails sounded like gunshots. Wind howled in the rigging.

Few of the Pilgrim adults and none of the children ventured up on deck. The waves washed twenty-seven-year-old John Howland overboard. Luckily, he caught hold of some rigging and was rescued. Children had to be protected from the waves and kept from annoying the sailors. A sailor's job was difficult and dangerous. They were rough men who had no

*The Pilgrims aboard the* **Mayflower**,
*which carried 102 voyagers to the New World.*

patience with anyone who got in their way. Try to imagine living for nine and a half weeks in a smelly, smoky, cramped, crowded, cold, and wet basement that heaves and drops into the waves like a roller coaster out of control.

The storms became so bad that the crew wanted to turn back. They got into a violent argument with the Pilgrims, who insisted they keep going. The discussion ended when the captain decided that since they were halfway there, it made more sense to go forward than to turn around. The voyage continued.

Despite the horrible conditions, only two people died during the trip. One was a sailor who had been vicious and cruel to the Pilgrims. He told them they would all die, and he would take their money and possessions. The Pilgrims were taught to "turn the other cheek," so they answered him with soft words or simply ignored him. But his teasing must have terrified people who were already afraid and nervous. Then, without warning, the young sailor dropped dead of a strange and terrible disease. It was a shock to the other sailors. Superstitious men, they saw their friend's death as a warning from God. From then on they left the Pilgrims alone. The only Pilgrim to die was Dr. Fuller's servant, William Butten. What he died of is not known. He was buried at sea. All the rest of the people on board ship arrived safely, as did the dogs, cats, and pet birds. There was even a baby born at sea. He was named Oceanus.

Finally, after weeks of storms and sickness, land was sighted. They had reached the New World. It was a dark and forbidding looking place, but to the storm-tossed Pilgrims it was a beautiful sight. As William Bradford recorded in his journal, "We were not a little joyful."

# 5

# DEATH IN THE WILDERNESS

It was autumn when the Pilgrims finally reached the New World. The coastline looked barren, cold, and harsh. William Bradford described it as "a hideous and desolate wilderness, full of wild beasts and wild men. . . . For summer being done, all things stand upon them with a weatherbeaten face, and the whole country, full of woods and thickets, represented a wild and savage hue."

The Pilgrims had not reached Virginia, but were far to the north on Cape Cod. The harbor was good, and the ship anchored safely. But the Pilgrims had landed at a place the charter did not govern. Some of the passengers began to grumble and complain, saying that now that they had no government it would be chaos. The leaders immediately realized this could spell disaster for the little band. They had to stick together or perish. A meeting was called on board the ship, and the famous Mayflower Compact was drawn up. Every head of household signed it. The compact bound them together by stating that they had the power to enact their own laws and enforce them. Each person swore to obey the laws. John Carver

*The signing of the "Mayflower Compact"*

On Monday, November 13, 1620, the women and
children went ashore for the first time.

was elected governor and the meeting ended. It was the first time on American soil that a group of free men and women drew up laws to govern themselves. And the laws were the first that said the majority should rule.

After this, fifteen or sixteen men volunteered to go ashore and explore. They saw no signs of Indians. They reported that there were vast forests and no sweet water. Sunday was the first full day on the shores of the New World, but since it was the Lord's Day no work was done. Instead, the Pilgrims prayed. The prayers probably were ones of thanksgiving for the Lord's grace in steering them so far in safety. That Sunday, November 12, 1620, might be said to be the first Thanksgiving, although there were no games or feasts. Yet the Pilgrims were undoubtedly truly thankful to be alive and safe from the perils of the sea.

On Monday, the women went ashore to wash the foul-smelling clothes and bedding. The children and dogs were also allowed off the ship, and they raced up and down the beach, glad to be free to move around at last. Sentries were posted to watch for Indians. The Pilgrims found clams and ate them hungrily, delighted to have fresh food after the spoiled, bug-filled food aboard ship. Unfortunately, they knew nothing about cooking clams because they had never seen them before. And so those who ate them were violently ill. Months later the Indians would teach them how to cook clams and other shellfish.

Thus began the first hard winter for the Pilgrims. They lived on the *Mayflower*. Launching a small boat into the water to go ashore was a difficult task. But nevertheless, scouting parties, many under the leadership of Captain Miles Standish, explored the land for weeks searching for a suitable place to build the settlement. They found signs of Indians, all of whom had apparently hidden at the sight of the strange men and the boat. Then the Pilgrims came to an abandoned Indian village. Here they made a wonderful discovery. Corn! They took it back to the ship, vowing to pay the Indians for it if they ever found them. (The Pilgrims did eventually repay the Indians about six months later.) Not all of the Indians were afraid of the white men and their guns, however. The party was attacked once. Captain Standish ordered his men to fire, and the Indians were scared away. But the Pilgrims realized they were in danger.

Yet it was one of the children who nearly brought the entire expedition to a terrible end. Young Francis Billington, bored with roaming around the ship, decided to go below and get out his father's guns and gunpowder. The fourteen-year-old boy first experimented with making firecrackers. These didn't go off, but he managed to spill gunpowder all over the deck. Then he fired two of his father's muskets and a fowling piece. Why he didn't blow up the entire ship is a mystery. The startled adults rushed to his cabin, and Francis was in trouble. He was not hurt, at least by the explosives. What his parents said and did to him later is not known—but the Bible states that "to spare the rod" spoils the child.

In December, the *Mayflower* moved to a sheltered cove near the place that became known as Plymouth Rock. The exploring party first set foot on Plymouth Rock on Monday, December 11, 1620. Bradford described the historic sight with little enthusiasm. It was "a place [they supposed] fit for situation. At least it was the best they could find." The *Mayflower* came around the following Saturday. It was not a happy occasion for William Bradford. His wife, Dorothy, had fallen overboard and drowned.

*The Pilgrims hold a Sunday worship service.*

There were no long speeches as the Pilgrims stepped onto the now famous rock. They were too exhausted from trying to survive. The stores had to be unloaded from the vessel and some sort of shelter constructed. The water was icy cold, and rowing back to the ship time after time was tiring, back-breaking work. The men were soon chilled to the bone. Many caught colds that eventually led to pneumonia and death.

The Pilgrims built a common dwelling house, called the Common House, first. It was 20 square feet (1.9 sq m) and had a few windows covered with oil paper. Most of the people lived in the Common House while the rest lived in dugouts covered with sod. Next they began to lay out the town—nineteen plots of land. They saw no Indians. There was some wild game and vegetation in the forest. But the Pilgrims were afraid to try the strange berries and plants they found. Scurvy and then pneumonia spread. Six people died in December, eight in January, seventeen in February, and thirteen in March. The *Mayflower* lost nearly half its ship's crew. Almost everyone got sick. Those who were able to walk, however weak they were, helped those who couldn't. It was a sad and terrible time, but somehow the Pilgrims struggled through it. Without their selfless labors, none of them would have survived. Even the rough sailors were amazed to see those they had cruelly teased and despised come to their aid when they fell sick—when their own comrades refused to tend them.

The dead were buried in secret at night, so the Indians, who had stolen some tools, would not guess how weak the colony was. With March and the coming of spring, the worst was over, although the colonists did not know it at the time.

One early spring day an Indian appeared in camp. He walked straight up to them and began to speak—in English!

The Pilgrims had found their first friend.

# 6

# NEW FRIENDS

The Indian's name was Samoset. He came from Maine where he had met Englishmen in fishing vessels. The Pilgrims welcomed him and gave him a red coat. (He was wearing very little and the Pilgrims were embarrassed at his nakedness.) He asked for food and beer, and they gave him both. In return, Samoset told the Pilgrims that the local Indians were peaceful. He offered to introduce them to their chief—the great Massasoit. He said there was another Indian living with Massasoit who spoke English. This Indian's name was Squanto.

Samoset left. Within a few days he returned with Massasoit and some of his tribe members. The first meeting of the Pilgrims and the Indians was held with great solemnity. Governor Carver kissed the chief's hand, and the Indian embraced Carver. The Pilgrims and the Indians made a treaty that day which was kept, with occasional lapses, for sixty years.

The story of Squanto is truly an adventure. He had been taken to England by Captain George Wymouth in 1605. He lived in England for several years and learned to speak English. Returning to America in 1614 as an interpreter for Captain John Smith, Squanto was kidnapped by a traitorous ship's cap-

*Samoset visits the Pilgrims.*

tain. He and sixteen other Indians were taken to Spain where they were sold in the slave market. Some were sent to Africa and never heard from again. Squanto was bought by some Spanish friars as a servant and was fairly well-treated. He escaped to London and once again sailed for America. He jumped ship and went back to his tribe. He found that all of his people had gotten sick and died. Roaming alone through the countryside, he decided to live with Massasoit.

Squanto had no bitter feeling toward white people after this poor treatment. Indeed, he became the Pilgrims' savior. Not only did he act as their interpreter with Massasoit, explaining many Indian ways and customs, but he taught them how to plant corn and other crops. He showed them the best places to fish and taught them how to cook the fish and strange plants and vegetables they found.

Thus, with the coming of spring, the Pilgrims lifted their heads after the bitter and deadly winter. They began to hope that they might survive after all. Wives and husbands had died, leaving widows, widowers, and orphans. Children had died as well. The small baby, Oceanus, born on ship, was dead. There were only fifty-four persons left to start the new American colony.

Interestingly enough, twenty-one of these people were under the age of sixteen. Almost half of our country's founders were children!

# 7

# THE FIRST
# THANKSGIVING

In April 1621, the *Mayflower* sailed back to England. It did not carry fish or furs or anything else to pay back the sponsors. The Pilgrims were on their own. Not one of them decided to return to their former homeland with the ship. They were committed to the new land.

Everyone helped to raise the crops that would determine life or death the next winter. Squanto showed them how to plant corn and they all worked in the corn fields—even Governor Carver. One hot day, he worked without a hat, and complained of a headache. Within days he was dead of sunstroke. Thirty-one-year-old William Bradford was elected governor. Edward Winslow, twenty-five, was the Indian ambassador, with thirty-five-year-old Stephen Hopkins as his assistant. Miles Standish, thirty-five, was the military captain. William Brewster was the pastor.

Spring and summer of 1621 were beautiful. The crops grew at a rate that astonished the Pilgrims. Squanto taught them how to fish and hunt and how to cook what they caught. The other Indians were friendly—too friendly, in fact. They continually dropped by the hospitable Pilgrim camp and cheerfully ate the food meant for winter. Finally the Pilgrims politely sent a messenger to Massasoit asking him to keep his people at home.

That summer one of the Billington boys got into trouble. Francis's little brother, John, wandered off into the woods and disappeared. A search party set out after him. Soon, however, Massasoit signaled that the boy had been found. He was being relayed from one Indian outpost to the next on his way home. John Billington returned safely and was, no doubt, a hero to the other children. He came back in the arms of an Indian brave "with a great train of warriors" as an escort. The boy was decorated with beads and probably enjoyed his escapade a great deal!

Then autumn arrived. The Pilgrim colony had survived its first year, although there were many secret graves of friends and loved ones. But now there was plenty of food. The woods were fiery in their autumn color and filled with game. Crops were harvested. Winter no longer held the threat of death that it had the year before. Eleven good houses stood safe and strong to shelter the families.

The Pilgrims made peace with the Indians and had learned a great deal from their new friends. It was only fitting that they decided to celebrate to mark the momentous first year of the colony's survival. They held a harvest festival.

This festival was not a religious ceremony, as has sometimes been assumed. The Pilgrims would have marked a religious holiday with solemn prayer and fasting, certainly not the games and feasting of that first Thanksgiving. There were prayers, undoubtedly, for prayer was a part of their everyday life. But it was not a solemn occasion.

The date of the first Thanksgiving is not known. It was sometime between the first of October and the first of November. When all the crops were gathered in, Governor Bradford sent four men out "fowling" and they killed enough birds— ducks, geese, and the traditional turkey—to "feed the Company almost a week." The Pilgrims invited their friends, the Indians, and Massasoit arrived with ninety braves! The guests outnumbered the hosts, but the Pilgrims fed them all in gratitude for their help.

The Indians were accustomed to harvest festivals. They celebrated the Green Corn Dance every year. How the Wampanoag tribe celebrated the festival is not known; the Pilgrims did not leave any record. But for other Indian tribes it was a rite of renewal in which old clothes and other items not fit for use were burned. The Green Corn Dance lasted for four days. The Indians feasted on new corn to begin a fresh new year.

The Indians killed five deer and presented them to Bradford on that first Thanksgiving. In addition to the venison, the Pilgrims and Indians ate the fowl they had killed plus eels, clams, lobsters, and oysters. There were wild plums, gooseberries, strawberries, and cherries, which had been dried according to Indian instruction. They drank wine made from their own grapes. They had wheat to make biscuits and bread. There was corn bread, hoecakes, and Indian pudding made with cornmeal and molasses. There may have even been popcorn balls, for the Indians popped the corn in earthen jars over the coals and then poured maple syrup over it.

There was probably not any cranberry sauce for that first Thanksgiving feast. The Pilgrims had no sugar to make either sauce or jelly, and although the bitter red berries grew abundantly, they are not mentioned in the Pilgrim journals or letters. There was no pumpkin pie, either. Even though the Indians raised pumpkins, the Pilgrims may have been reluctant to eat the strange looking vegetable. The Indians probably

*The first Thanksgiving in America*

cooked whole pumpkins, hollowed out and filled with butter, in the coals of a fire.

The feasting and celebrating lasted three days. Indians danced. The Pilgrims played games such as stool ball. They showed off their marksmanship with the guns, which the Indians admired, but refused to handle. Captain Standish marched his small band of men about in parade, and they blew their bugles, instruments which impressed the Indians almost as much as the noisy guns. The chill winds reminded Pilgrim and Indian alike that the harsh winter was coming. The feasting and the games ended. The Indians returned to their camp. The Pilgrims settled in to survive another winter. Perhaps they were a little worried, for the Indians had eaten up more food than they had expected. But on November 10 they had another reason to celebrate. A ship sailed into the harbor. It was the first contact the Pilgrims had had with their native land for sixty-two weeks.

The ship was the *Fortune*. It carried thirty-five passengers and not much else, having only enough food to reach Virginia. It also brought William Brewster's oldest son, Jonathan, and an angry letter from the sponsors back in England. They wanted to know why the *Mayflower* had been sent back empty, and they asked for their money.

Brewster wrote back telling of their hardships and asking for their support. The *Fortune* left for England two weeks later, leaving the Pilgrims with more mouths to feed and no additional food or supplies except some clothing.

# 8

# THANKSGIVING IN THE COLONIES

The Pilgrims did not hold another Thanksgiving celebration until July 30, 1623. This has been called by some the first official Thanksgiving because Governor Bradford set it aside as a special day.

The winter of 1622 had been terribly severe and came after a skimpy harvest. Legend says that the Pilgrims, not as skilled in growing corn as the Indians, were reduced to eating only five grains per person per day.

More ships came from England, bringing new colonists but not much more in the way of supplies. Some of the new people proved to be troublemakers. They were selfish and greedy. They stole from the Indians, and the small colony lived under the constant fear of an attack. However, the spring of 1623 seemed promising. The crops were planted, and at least there were more people to work the fields.

Then a drought set in. For months there was no rain, only the beating sun. The crops withered, and it seemed as though there might be no food at all for winter. Finally the governor assembled the people and held a day of fasting and prayer for rain.

*During their first year in Plymouth,*
*the Pilgrims' rations were reduced to only*
*five grains of corn daily for each person.*

And it rained! The crops lived, and the governor proclaimed a day of Thanksgiving in July. Then two more ships landed, carrying old friends from Leyden! Friends who never thought they'd see one another again were reunited.

But it was a sad meeting. Bradford wrote that the Leyden Pilgrims were shocked by the appearance of those still alive in the little colony, who "were ragged in apparel and some little better than half naked. . . . The best dish they could present to their friends was a lobster or a piece of fish without bread or anything else but a cup of fair spring water." Many of the newcomers burst into tears, and others said they wished they had never come.

The rains brought a better-than-expected harvest, however. That fall the harvest festival was celebrated again, along with the wedding of William Bradford and Alice Southworth. There was venison, grapes, plums, nuts, pigs, and hens on that Thanksgiving. Massasoit came, bringing 120 braves, deer, and a turkey.

The custom of the Pilgrim harvest festival was established, and it spread to other American colonies. The Thanksgiving festival was held on a local basis, however, at different times in different places for different reasons. One Thanksgiving was celebrated in Boston in 1630 after the safe arrival of friends from Europe. Another was held in Connecticut in 1655 "on the last Wednesday of October . . . for the blessing of the fruits of the earth." Each colony proclaimed its own Thanksgiving Day, and cities held them whenever they had something to celebrate.

Thanksgiving was not forgotten during the Revolutionary War, though sometimes during the darker days of the war, there seemed little to be thankful for. An account of a Thanksgiving Day written in 1779 reads: "Of course we could have no Roast Beef. None of us have tasted Beef this three years back as it all must go to the Army, & too little they get, poor fellows." But there was venison, turkey, goose, and duck, and many families were together. This meant a great deal, even if "neither Love nor [paper] Money could buy Raisins . . ." and dried cherries had to be used in the mince pies.

When the war was over and the thirteen colonies had won their freedom from England, a day of national Thanksgiving was proposed to a joint session of the new Congress. Strangely enough, the proposal met with stiff resistance. They thought only the states should have the power to proclaim a Thanksgiving Day. Some said a national holiday was government interference in local affairs. Others said it was too early to celebrate. No one knew if the Constitution would work out. After much discussion and argument, the resolution was passed by both the House and Senate. President George Washington issued the First National Thanksgiving Proclamation, setting Thursday, November 26, 1789, as the day. The Proclamation reads, in part:

*Now therefore I do recommend and assign Thursday the 26th day of November next to be devoted by the People of these States to the service of that great and glorious Being, who is the beneficent Author of all that good that was, that is, or that will be—That we may then all unite in rendering unto Him our sincere and humble thanks—for His kind care and protection of the People of this country previous to their becoming a Nation—for the signal and manifold mercies, and the favorable interpositions of his providence, which we experienced in the course and conclusion of the last war.*

# 9

# A NATIONAL DAY
# OF THANKS

The idea of a national Thanksgiving Day did not catch on, however. Thomas Jefferson, our third president, believed the harvest festival was a pagan celebration. Various governors tried establishing a statewide holiday, but it was difficult to get everyone in even one state to agree upon a fixed date.

Some farmers celebrated, as had the early English, when the last load of grain was carried into the barn. These celebrations were different in practically every township. The Puritans believed thanksgiving days should be set according to the will of God and not politicians. Therefore, they ignored legal holidays and held their own. One city postponed a legally proclaimed Thanksgiving Day for a week because no molasses had arrived and the women could not bake without it!

But Thanksgiving Days were still being celebrated. The pioneers, moving like the Pilgrims into new and strange lands, carried the tradition with them. More and more people wanted a national day of Thanksgiving to be set aside by the federal government.

One woman decided to do something about it. Her name was Sarah Josepha Hale. She was an author and in 1837 became editor of a famous women's magazine called *Godey's Lady's Book*. She wrote hundreds of letters to influential people all over the country urging them to push for a national Thanksgiving Day holiday. Her magazine carried editorials about it, and she even included stories about traditional Thanksgiving Day celebrations in her novels.

When the nation was faced with civil war, Mrs. Hale stated that if "every state would join in Union thanksgiving . . . would it not be a renewed pledge of love and loyalty . . . ?" But the Civil War came and the nation was torn apart. In 1861, Mrs. Hale asked that each side lay down its arms for one day and remember that they had much to be thankful for.

No one listened. The war dragged on. There seemed to be no reason to celebrate.

Then, in 1863, President Abraham Lincoln saw that the war was nearing an end. He had already proclaimed a national day of Thanksgiving to celebrate the Union victory at the Battle of Gettysburg, but this was not the harvest festival celebration that Mrs. Hale was calling for.

She may have visited Lincoln personally to plead for her cause. In any case, President Lincoln finally proclaimed a national harvest festival to be held the last Thursday of November. In his proclamation he reminded the war-torn country they still had much to be thankful for. It is important to note that this proclamation extended to *every* American— even those in states who were fighting the Union:

> It has seemed to me fit and proper that they [all that which Americans are blessed with] should be solemnly, reverently, and gratefully acknowledged, as with one heart and one voice, by the whole American people, I do therefore invite

*my fellow-citizens in every part of the United States, and also those who are at sea, and those who are sojourning in foreign lands, to set apart and observe the last Thursday of November next as a day of thanksgiving and praise.*

Thus, Thanksgiving became a legal holiday. Eventually the war came to an end. The nation was united, and people had much to be thankful for. Lincoln's assassination almost stopped celebration of another Thanksgiving, but so many groups called for it that President Andrew Johnson issued the proclamation. Presidents continued the tradition, officially proclaiming the holiday and setting it for the fourth Thursday of November. At first, some church groups questioned the right of the federal government to proclaim what they saw as a religious holiday, but eventually almost everyone accepted it.

Thanksgivings were celebrated in a manner very similar to the Pilgrims. There was turkey and lots of good food to eat. Cranberries and pumpkins represented the fruits of the harvest. Thanksgiving also became the official start of the Christmas season—and that caused some trouble.

From 1939 through 1941, President Franklin Roosevelt proclaimed a Thanksgiving Day, but he proclaimed it for the *third* Thursday in November instead of the fourth. This was because merchants had complained that they didn't have enough time to sell their Christmas merchandise in the short time between Thanksgiving and Christmas when Thanksgiving was held at the end of the month.

Odd as it may seem, this change of date threw the country into turmoil! It even became a political issue. Republicans blasted the Democrats (Roosevelt was a Democrat) for going against tradition. They even harked back to the days of the

Pilgrim fathers, even though no one knows exactly when they celebrated Thanksgiving. Democrats supported their president, stating that since the economy was still suffering from the depression, the new date was much more practical. Colleges that had already scheduled football games for the traditional date were furious. Families were divided on the issue. Some wanted the new date, some wanted the old. Many families ended up having two Thanksgiving Day celebrations a week apart! After two years of confusion and turmoil, Roosevelt reversed his decision. Thanksgiving has been held on the fourth Thursday of November ever since.

# 10

# THANKSGIVING TODAY

Thanksgiving is one of the few American holidays that different ethnic groups celebrate in more or less the same way. It is one of the only holidays the Indians feel is as much theirs as it is the descendants of all the "pilgrims" who came to America. And it is one of the few holidays that has changed very little since its beginnings. Our ancestors would not recognize Christmas as we celebrate it today, but they would instantly know the harvest festival.

There is still feasting on traditional foods. Families gather together to give thanks for the blessings they have received during the year. Thanksgiving is a special time to remember loved ones far away. It is a time for games, too. Just as the Pilgrims played stool ball, we watch football games on television and play our own games outdoors.

Thanksgiving is a time for storytelling, too. Children eagerly gather around parents and grandparents to listen to stories about Thanksgivings past, just as the Pilgrim children might have listened to stories told by their fathers and mothers and the Indians. Our stories might be a little different, but they still remind us of our heritage.

Thanksgiving is also the beginning of the Christmas season. During the 1920s, Macy's department store in New York began celebrating Thanksgiving with a parade to mark the arrival of Santa Claus. The Macy's Thanksgiving Day Parade has been an important tradition for over fifty-five years. Floats, championship marching bands from all over the country, celebrities from stage and screen, and giant balloons featuring popular cartoon and holiday figures all parade down Broadway.

Balloons, first designed in 1927, were the creation of puppeteer and cartoonist, Tony Sarg. In the 1930s another famous puppeteer, Bill Baird, assisted in designing the figures that float down the streets of New York.

The Walt Disney studios created the popular Mickey Mouse and Pluto balloons in 1934. There have been a total of ninety-two balloon characters, including Bullwinkle the Moose, Superman, turkeys, and more. The parade was televised nationally in 1955 for the first time, and since then, over one and a half billion people have seen it.

Wherever Americans go, they will take the celebration of Thanksgiving Day with them. Perhaps in the future, a small colony, not unlike our Pilgrim ancestors, will gather around a table on some distant planet to thank God for His blessings. Possibly some strange and friendly alien race will be invited to participate.

The small colony will recall that, centuries ago, the Pilgrims risked everything they had, to worship God in their own way. They will remember how the Pilgrims survived terrible

*Macy's annual Thanksgiving Day*
*Parade in New York*

conditions in a strange land, established peaceful relations with the Indians, and willingly learned from them.

President George Washington's second Thanksgiving Day proclamation sums up our reasons for celebrating this holiday:

> *When we review the calamities which afflict so many other nations, the present condition of the United States affords much matter of consolation and satisfaction.... In such state of things it is in an especial manner our duty as a people, with devout reverence and affectionate gratitude, to acknowledge our many and great obligations to Almighty God and to implore Him to continue and confirm the blessings we experience.*

# 11

# THANKSGIVING FUN

## GAMES

What did the Pilgrim children do during those nine and one-half weeks crowded aboard the *Mayflower*? Remember, they were not allowed above deck, nor was there any room for running around or playing games that involved a great deal of space. There were sick people, too, whom the children had to be careful not to disturb. So, the children probably studied their lessons, particularly Bible lessons and Bible stories. They also played quiet games. You can play some of these games on the way to your traditional Thanksgiving Day dinner.

### Bird, Beast, or Fish

One child is chosen as the leader. He or she points to another child and says either "Bird" or "Beast" or "Fish." The child selected must quickly give the name of an animal in that category before the leader counts to ten. Names of animals cannot be repeated. If the child cannot think of one, he or she loses and is out of the game. The game gets harder and harder as more of the common animals are used up.

EXAMPLE:

Leader points to someone and calls out, "Fish."
(Leader begins to count to ten.)
The person pointed to says "Trout" before the leader finishes
    counting.
Leader points to someone else. "Beast," he or she says.
(Leader begins to count to ten.)
"Horse," answers the person quickly. (Neither "Horse" nor
    "Trout" can be used again.)

The game continues until everyone has missed. The last person
    left is the new leader.

## Even/Odd

Another early game the Pilgrim children might have played is
called Even/Odd. One person hides several small objects in his
hand. These could be dried beans or peas, beads, or marbles.
The other player has to guess whether the number of hidden
objects is even or odd.

## Twenty Questions

Popular today, this was another game Pilgrim children were
familiar with. One person tells the other player that he or she is
thinking of an object, and then must tell whether it is "animal,
vegetable, or mineral." The rest of the players then ask questions about this object—questions that can be answered "yes,"
"no," or "I don't know." Players can work together to get the
answer to the question. When someone knows the name of the
object he or she can whisper it to the leader, who will then tell
whether the answer is right or wrong. Anyone who doesn't
guess the object in twenty questions loses the game.

## Stool Ball

Games were an important part of the first Thanksgiving festivals. Stool ball is a game the Pilgrims probably played on that first Thanksgiving. Several variations of this game exist. Some say the game was a kind of croquet in which the players tried to hit the ball through the legs of a stool. Here is a type of stool ball you can play:

Place a three-legged stool in a large open space such as your backyard or the playground. One person, chosen to defend the stool, stands in front of it with a stick. The other players stand behind a line drawn ten steps away from the stool. Each player takes a turn trying to knock the stool down by throwing a ball at it. The ball should be the size of a soccer or kick ball. The defender must knock the ball away with the stick before it hits the stool. The defender can also kick the ball away, but cannot use his or her hands. The person who succeeds in knocking the stool over is the new defender.

This game may be played in teams as well, with each team trying to defend their own stool and attempting to knock the other team's stool over at the same time. Use only one ball. The winner is the team that keeps the stool upright the longest.

## Corn Game

The corn game brings to mind the hard winter when the Pilgrims lived on only five grains of corn per day.

This game should be played with a large group of children, perhaps your classmates or scout troop. An adult hides five ears of corn around the room or the house. The children then race to see who can find the ears first. After the corn is cooked, the five people who found the corn have a contest to see who can eat the corn the fastest.

*Pumpkin Roll*

This hilarious game involves the largest pumpkins you can find (or afford). The object of the game is to see who can roll a pumpkin, turned over on its side, past the finish line first. Older children can use a stick. Smaller children can roll the pumpkin with their hands. Since lumpy pumpkins won't roll in a straight line, contestants can end up all over the field trying to get to the finish line! This game may also be played as a relay race. Two teams—each divided into two groups—roll their pumpkin back and forth until one team finishes.

## THINGS TO MAKE

*Cranberry Stringing Contest*

We think of this as a Christmas custom, but Midwestern children used to have cranberry stringing contests on Thanksgiving Day. Each child is given a thread 20 inches (50.8 cm) long and a needle. The first child who strings all the cranberries onto the thread is the winner. You can wear the cranberry necklaces during the day, but wear old clothes—the cranberries stain. You might want to alternate the cranberries with popcorn. The strings can be hung on the Christmas tree or used to feed the birds.

*Friendship Pins*

The Indians decorated their clothing with beautiful designs made of porcupine quills dyed many different colors. Like face painting, the designs had very special meanings for the Indians.

When traders came to the New World from Europe, they brought colored beads. The beads were highly prized by the Indians because they were prettier and easier to work with than porcupine quills. You can decorate your clothing and shoes with these colorful, beaded friendship pins and give them to your friends. They are fun, easy to make, and can be worn on tennis shoes or necklaces.

Take a safety pin of any size, and slide beads of different colors down the open arm of the safety pin. You can purchase safety pins and beads in fabric stores. Make certain the beads are large enough to fit the safety pin. Generally, if you use the small gold safety pins, nearly any size bead will fit. Wear the pins on the laces of your tennis shoes, hang them from a chain around your neck, or pin them to the collar of your shirt. You can have lots of fun making and exchanging the colorful pins.

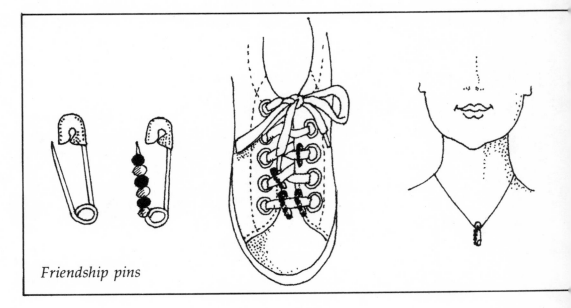

*Friendship pins*

## THINGS TO DO

### Indian Visitors

Years ago children in the East dressed as Indians and painted their faces on Thanksgiving. They went from door to door asking for treats to celebrate the arrival of the Indians among the Pilgrims.

### Indian Face Painting

Indians painted their faces for many different reasons. Face paint was used during war to express happiness or grief, and for special celebrations. The design the Indian chose was something very personal and special. The Indian was inspired by dreams, forces of nature, and great events.

Think about something that has special meaning to you. Do you like to be outdoors in the sunshine? If so, you may want to paint a bright yellow sun on your cheek. Are you frightened by lightning? Paint a white zigzag lightning streak on your face to show you will not be afraid when a storm hits.

You can use other designs just because they look scary—like three bright red stripes drawn across your nose from one side of your face to the other. Draw a bold blue stripe from the center of your forehead down your nose. Then draw three blue stripes across your cheeks.

The Indians used crushed berries, charcoal, dirt and clay, blood, and some other natural materials to make paint. You might try some of these (but not blood!), if you have them available and an adult helps. You can get charcoal out of the fireplace, for example. There are many inexpensive makeup kits sold in dime stores for Halloween which are excellent for face painting.

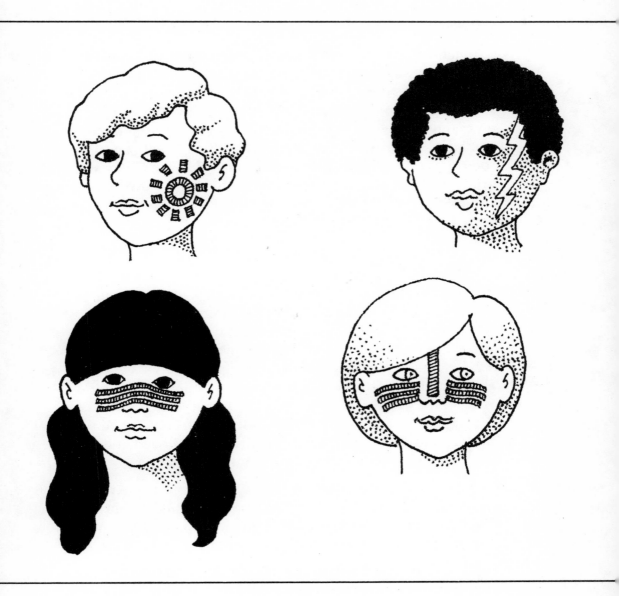

*Indian face painting*

*Storytelling*

Storytelling has always been a traditional part of Thanksgiving. Your grandparents and great-grandparents can tell you about Thanksgivings during the Depression and during the World Wars. Soldiers often came up with unique and sometimes touching ways to celebrate the holiday far from home. If you have aunts and uncles visiting, ask them to tell you stories about your own parents and what they did when they were little. You might want to record these stories on a cassette tape and play it back the next Thanksgiving. Or put the stories in a diary like the one William Bradford kept.

*Thanksgiving on Mars*

William Bradford kept a journal, or a diary, of the day-to-day life of the Pilgrims. The diary and the letters sent to England by other members of the colony have told us much about the Pilgrims, the voyage, their problems, the way they lived, and how they celebrated that first Thanksgiving. Imagine what a future Thanksgiving might be like for the first American colony on Mars. Write about this in the form of a journal. You will need to do a little research about Mars to find out about the climate and conditions on the planet. Then let your imagination go! Here are some things you might want to include:

1. What is Mars like? What is the average temperature? What kind of shelters would you have to build to survive? What does the planet look like? If you looked out the window of your spaceship, what would you see first?

2. What would you have to eat for your Martian Thanksgiving dinner? Did you bring the food with you? If you grew it on Mars, what kinds of weird foods might you have to eat?

3. What did you take with you to Mars? What kinds of clothes are you wearing? Did you bring your dog or cat? How does your pet like Mars? Did you bring along your favorite books? What are their titles? Remember—you can't buy books on Mars. (You must decide on your very favorites because you don't have room to pack too many.)

4. Scientists tell us you won't find intelligent life on Mars. But it would be fun to pretend you and your group of colonists discovered Martians who helped you out just as the Indians helped the Pilgrims. What would the Martians be like? You would invite them to Thanksgiving dinner, of course. How would you explain Thanksgiving to them? Would they be likely to celebrate something similar?

## RECIPES

### Turkey

The traditional turkey should be prepared by adults. But you can learn a great deal by watching, if you are careful not to get in the way. Here is a turkey recipe from 1881:

> *Get your turkey six weeks before you need it; put him in a coop just large enough to let him walk, or in a small yard; give him walnuts—one the first day, and increase everyday until you kill him, [feeding] him twice with cornmeal dough each day, in which you put a little chopped onion and celery . . . [kill the turkey and dress it] . . . pour boiling water inside and outside [the turkey] to cleanse and plump it; then roast it . . . basting all the time. It will be splendid, served with a nice piece of ham and cranberry sauce.*

## Indian Pudding

INGREDIENTS:

4 cups milk
2/3 cup dark molasses
2/3 cup yellow cornmeal
1/3 cup sugar
1 teaspoon salt
3/4 teaspoon cinnamon
3/4 teaspoon nutmeg
3/4 teaspoon ground ginger
1/4 cup butter or margarine

Heat oven to 300 degrees. Grease a 2-quart casserole. In one bowl, mix the cornmeal, sugar, salt, cinnamon, nutmeg, and ginger. Set aside. Heat 3 cups of the milk and the molasses over low heat, stirring to keep milk from burning. Slowly stir the cornmeal mixture into the hot milk. Add the butter. Cook over low heat, stirring constantly, about ten minutes or until the mixture thickens.

Pour into the casserole. Pour 1 cup of milk over the pudding. Do not stir! Bake three hours. Serve with maple syrup, ice cream, or whipping cream.

## Roozle's Rolls

These are a tradition from my own family. My little sister ate so many we named them after her. (Roozle is her nickname; her real name is Terry.) When we were older, my mother let us make them. The kitchen always ended up covered with flour, but it was worth it! Make these the day before Thanksgiving.

You will need one big bowl and two little bowls.

INGREDIENTS:

3/4 cup solid shortening
1 cup boiling water
3 packages dry yeast
1/2 cup warm water
2 eggs
3/4 cup sugar
2 teaspoons salt
1 cup cold water
7 1/2 cups flour

Put the shortening in one small bowl. Pour the boiling water over it and stir until the shortening dissolves. In the other bowl put 3 packages of dry yeast into the warm water. (Be certain it is *not hot*! Hot water will kill the yeast.) Put these two bowls to one side. In the big bowl, mix 2 eggs, the sugar, salt, and cold water. Beat with an electric beater until the mixture is the color of pale lemons. Next add the shortening and then the yeast. Stir together. Now you are ready to add the flour. (Count the cups of flour as you add them. Have someone mark them down as you call them out.) Add the flour slowly. Stir until all the flour is completely mixed. Cover the bowl, and put it in the refrigerator.

The dough will rise overnight. You will be amazed when you see it in the morning! In fact, you will have so much dough you may not want to use it all at once. Don't worry—the dough will keep in the refrigerator for one week. (This recipe makes 64 rolls.)

On Thanksgiving Day, take out the dough three hours before dinner. Decide how much you want to use. Put the rest back in the refrigerator. Get out your rolling pin. Put flour on the rolling pin and on a bread board (or another flat surface).

Roll the dough until it is flat (about ¼″—6 cm—thick) and in the shape of a circle. Now cut the dough into triangles, or wedges. Take one piece and roll it up, starting at the wide end. Roll up all the others just like it, and put them on a greased cookie sheet. Let the rolls rise in a warm place for three hours.

Preheat the oven to 425 degrees. Bake the rolls for ten minutes or until golden brown. (The rolls may be baked after the turkey is out of the oven. It will give you something to do while the turkey is being carved.)

*Frozen Fruit Salad*

This frozen fruit salad is easy to make, and the tartness of the pineapple tastes good with the turkey. Use colored marshmallows for this holiday dish that is pretty and delicious!

INGREDIENTS:

1 3-ounce package of cream cheese
1 cup mayonnaise
1 4-ounce can crushed pineapple and 2 tablespoons of its juice
1½ cups small marshmallows, cut in half
1 cup whipping cream

Soften the cream cheese. (Let it sit in a bowl until it is soft enough to stir with a spoon.) Mix the mayonnaise into the cream cheese. Add the pineapple, the pineapple juice, and the marshmallows. Stir all the ingredients together. Whip the cream until it stands up in white mountains. Mix the whipped cream into the marshmallow mixture. Pour into a mold (for a pretty salad), making certain the mold has been oiled first. Freeze. Serves eight.

# BIBLIOGRAPHY

*Mourt's Relation.* A journal of the pilgrims at Plymouth, edited from the original printing of 1622, with introduction and notes, by Dwight B. Heath. New York: Corinth Books, 1963.

Bradford, William. *Of Plymouth Plantation.* New York: Random House, 1952.

Caffrey, Kate. *The Mayflower.* New York: Stein and Day, 1974.

Lineon, Ralph and Adelin. *We Gather Together.* New York: Henry Schuman, 1949.

Love, W. DeLoss. *The Fast and Thanksgiving Days of New England.* Boston and New York: Houghton, Mifflin, 1895.

Sickel, H. S. J. *Thanksgiving: Its Source, Philosophy, and History with All National Proclamations and Analytical Study Thereof.* Philadelphia: Press of International Printing Company, 1940.

Stella, Jacques. *Games and Pastimes of Childhood.* New York: Dover Publications, 1969.

Strobell, Adah Parker. "Like It Was." *Bicentennial Games 'n Fun Handbook.* Washington: Acropolis Books, 1975.

# INDEX